DIGITAL MARKETING FOR BEGINNERS

The Definitive 2025 Guide to Understanding Personal Brand and Social Media

Rex Goldstein

CONTENTS

INTRODUCTION: THE POWER OF DIGITAL MARKETING

Imagine a world where you can share your passion, expertise, and unique perspective with millions of people across the globe—all from the comfort of your home. A world where you can turn your creativity into a lucrative business, achieve financial independence, and design a lifestyle that offers flexibility and freedom. Welcome to digital marketing.

A New Era of Opportunity

In the 2020s, digital marketing stands as one of the most powerful and accessible avenues for achieving personal and financial growth. The barriers to entry are low, the opportunities are vast, and the potential for success is limited only by your imagination and dedication. Whether you're an aspiring entrepreneur, a creative professional, or someone looking to make a meaningful impact, digital marketing provides the tools and platforms to turn your dreams into reality.

The Why Behind
Digital Marketing

Leveraging Your Unique Voice

At its core, digital marketing is about communication. It's about sharing your story, your knowledge, and your passion with the world. Unlike traditional marketing methods, which often require significant capital and resources, digital marketing leverages the power of the internet to connect directly with audiences on a global scale. Your unique voice becomes your most valuable asset, allowing you to stand out in a crowded digital landscape.

Consider the example of a travel enthusiast who starts a blog to document their adventures. By sharing authentic stories, stunning photos, and practical tips, they can attract a dedicated following of like-minded individuals. Over time, this blog can evolve into a platform that generates income through advertising, sponsorships, and affiliate marketing. What began as a personal passion transforms into a thriving business, all driven by the power of a unique voice.

Minimal Start-Up Costs

One of the most compelling aspects of digital marketing is its affordability. Unlike traditional businesses that require substantial upfront investments, digital marketing primarily requires time, creativity, and dedication. Basic equipment such as a computer, a smartphone, and an internet connection are often sufficient to get started. There are numerous free or low-cost tools and resources available to help you create and distribute content, analyze performance, and engage with your audience.

Take the example of a budding chef who wants to share their culinary creations with the world. With a smartphone to capture photos and videos, and free platforms like Instagram and YouTube to share content, they can build an audience without significant financial investment. As their following grows, opportunities for monetization through sponsorships, cooking classes, and product sales emerge, demonstrating the scalability of digital marketing efforts.

Achieving Financial Independence

In an era where traditional career paths are increasingly uncertain, digital marketing offers a viable path to financial independence. Traditional jobs often come with limitations: fixed salaries, rigid schedules, and geographic constraints. Digital marketing, on the other hand, offers unparalleled flexibility. You can work from anywhere, set your own hours, and scale your efforts according to your goals and lifestyle.

Starting as a side hustle, digital marketing can gradually evolve into a full-time career. Many successful digital marketers began their journeys while juggling other commitments, slowly building their brand and audience until they reached a tipping point. Once your digital presence is established and your income streams are consistent, you have the freedom to decide whether to transition to full-time digital marketing or maintain it as a lucrative side venture.

Flexibility And Growth Potential

The flexibility of digital marketing extends beyond just work hours and location. It also allows for continuous growth and adaptation. The digital landscape is dynamic, with new platforms, trends, and technologies emerging regularly. This constant evolution means that there are always new opportunities to explore and new ways to connect with your audience.

For example, social media platforms like TikTok, Instagram, and YouTube have created unprecedented opportunities for content creators to reach vast audiences. Each platform has its own unique features and user base, allowing you to tailor your content strategy to maximize engagement and growth. Additionally, the rise of influencer marketing has opened up new revenue streams, as brands increasingly seek authentic voices to promote their products and services.

From Side Hustle to Main Hustle

One of the most remarkable aspects of digital marketing is its potential for scalability. What starts as a small side project can grow into a significant source of income and even become your primary occupation. This scalability is driven by the ability to reach and engage with large audiences, create multiple income streams, and build a sustainable business model.

Consider the journey of an artist who begins by sharing their work on social media. Initially, they might sell a few pieces to friends and followers. As their audience grows, they can expand their offerings to include prints, merchandise, and commissioned work. Collaborations with brands, participation in art shows, and the launch of an online store can further boost their income. What started as a passion project evolves into a thriving art business, supported by a loyal and engaged audience.

Designing Your Life

At its best, digital marketing allows you to design a life that aligns with your values, passions, and goals. It offers the freedom to pursue what you love, connect with like-minded individuals, and make a meaningful impact. Whether you're looking to escape the 9-to-5 grind, achieve financial independence, or simply share your creativity with the world, digital marketing provides the tools and platforms to make it happen.

As you embark on this journey, remember that success in digital marketing requires patience, persistence, and a willingness to learn and adapt. The digital landscape is ever-changing, and staying ahead of trends and technologies is crucial for maintaining and growing your presence. However, with dedication and a clear vision, the possibilities are limitless.

Conclusion

Digital marketing is more than just a career; it's

a gateway to freedom, creativity, and financial independence. By leveraging your unique voice, taking advantage of minimal start-up costs, and embracing the flexibility and growth potential of the digital world, you can create a sustainable and fulfilling business. Whether you're just starting or looking to take your digital marketing efforts to the next level, this manual will provide you with the insights, strategies, and tools you need to succeed. Welcome to the exciting and dynamic world of digital marketing—let's begin this journey together.

PART 1: PERSONAL BRAND

The Value of a Personal Brand

In the world of digital marketing, your personal brand is your most valuable asset. It's the unique combination of your personality, values, expertise, and style that distinguishes you from others in your field. Your personal brand serves as your moat in the digital landscape. It creates a space that attracts and retains an audience, enabling you to build a thriving community and business.

Building Community

A strong personal brand is the foundation upon

which you can build a dedicated community. When people connect with your brand, they must feel a sense of belonging and trust. This connection is crucial for digital marketing success, as it leads to higher engagement, loyalty, and advocacy. Your community members are more likely to listen to your opinions, share your content, and purchase the products or services you recommend.

Illustrative Example: Casey Neistat

Casey Neistat, a filmmaker and YouTube personality, is an excellent example of someone who has built a robust personal brand. Neistat's content is characterized by his raw, authentic storytelling style and his adventurous spirit. He started by posting daily vlogs that offered a glimpse into his life, showcasing both the highs and lows. His authenticity and consistency resonated with viewers, leading to a dedicated following.

Neistat's personal brand is built on more than just his filmmaking skills. It's also about his values—his passion for creativity, his entrepreneurial spirit, and his willingness to take risks. This strong personal brand has allowed him to create a loyal community that not only consumes his content but also supports his external ventures.

When Neistat recommends a product or collaborates with a brand, his audience trusts his judgment because they feel a personal connection with him. This level of influence and trust is the hallmark of a strong personal brand.

Attracting Brand Partnerships

A compelling personal brand not only helps you connect with your audience but also makes you attractive to brands. Companies are increasingly looking for authentic voices to promote their products and services. They recognize that influencers with a strong personal brand can create more genuine and impactful endorsements compared to traditional advertising methods.

Illustrative Example: Chiara Ferragni

Chiara Ferragni, an Italian fashion influencer and entrepreneur, exemplifies how a strong personal brand can attract significant brand partnerships. Ferragni started her blog, The Blonde Salad, in 2009 and quickly gained a massive following.

Ferragni's personal brand is characterized by her fashion-forward approach, her glamorous lifestyle, and her entrepreneurial drive. As her influence grew, major fashion brands such as Dior, Louis Vuitton, and Chanel began seeking her out for collaborations. These partnerships were not just about product placements; they involved co-creating collections and exclusive lines, further solidifying her status as a fashion icon.

Ferragni's personal brand has also led to the

success of her own fashion line, which has become a multimillion-dollar business in its own right. Brands are willing to partner with her because they know her influence and authenticity resonate deeply with her audience.

Curating an Authentic Voice

In today's social media landscape, authenticity is more important than ever. Audiences are becoming increasingly savvy and can easily detect insincerity. The days of perfectly curated, highly polished content are waning. Instead, people are drawn to real, relatable, and imperfect stories. Your authentic voice is what sets you apart and makes you relatable to your audience. Users are seeking content that reflects real-life experiences, emotions, and challenges. They want to see the human side of influencers, not just the highlight reel. This represents a significant opportunity for digital marketers to connect with their audience on a deeper level.

Illustrative Example: Jenna Marbles

Jenna Marbles, a comedian and YouTube personality, became famous for her humorous and often self-deprecating content. Unlike many influencers who strive for perfection, Marbles embraced her quirks and imperfections. She posted videos in which she wore no makeup, showed her daily routines, and shared her struggles with mental health.

Marbles' authenticity resonated with millions of viewers, who appreciated her honesty and relatability. Her videos amassed billions of views, and she became one of the most subscribed-to channels on YouTube. Her influence extended beyond her comedic content; it created a sense of community where viewers felt seen and understood. In fact, although she has been off social media since 2020, she had such an authentic voice that even to this day, there are entire communities and subcommunities devoted to getting her back online.

The Power Of Relatability

Relatability is a key component of a strong personal brand. When your audience sees themselves in your stories and experiences, they are more likely to engage with your content and support your endeavors. This principle is rooted in the concept of social proof, where people look to others for cues on how to think and act.

Illustrative Example: Gary Vaynerchuk

Gary Vaynerchuk, an entrepreneur and social media influencer, has built his personal brand on relatability and practical advice. Vaynerchuk started by documenting his journey of growing his family's wine business, which resonated with aspiring entrepreneurs and business owners.

Vaynerchuk's content is characterized by his no-nonsense, candid style. He shares his successes and failures, offers practical tips, and engages with his audience through Q&A sessions and live interactions. This approach has made him highly relatable to his audience, who see him as a mentor and advisor.

When Vaynerchuk endorses a product or service, his audience trusts his opinion because they perceive him as genuine and relatable. This trust has allowed him to build a successful personal brand and expand his influence into various business ventures.

Developing Your Personal Brand

Building a personal brand is a strategic and ongoing process. It requires a clear understanding of who you are, what you stand for, and how you want to be perceived. Here are some essential steps to help you develop a compelling personal brand:

1. Define Your Brand Identity

Your brand identity is the essence of who you are and what you represent. It encompasses your values, mission, and unique qualities. To define your brand identity, ask yourself the following questions:
- What are my core values and beliefs?

- What makes me unique in my field?
- What do I want to be known for?
- How do I want to impact my audience?

Illustrative Example: Marie Forleo

Marie Forleo, a life coach, and entrepreneur, has built a personal brand centered around empowering individuals to achieve their goals. Forleo's brand identity is defined by her values of optimism, resilience, and personal growth. Her mission is to help people create a business and life they love.

Forleo's unique qualities, such as her energetic personality and motivational speaking style, set her apart in the personal development industry. By consistently communicating her values and mission through her content, Forleo has created a strong and recognizable personal brand.

2. Identify Your Target Audience

Knowing your target audience is crucial for creating content that resonates and engages. Consider the demographics, interests, and pain points of the people you want to reach. Understanding your audience allows you to tailor your content and messaging to their needs and preferences.

Illustrative Example: Pat Flynn

Pat Flynn, the founder of Smart Passive Income, has built his personal brand by focusing on aspiring entrepreneurs and online business owners. Flynn identified that his target audience consists of individuals seeking passive income opportunities and practical advice on building online businesses.

Flynn's content, which includes podcasts, blog posts, and online courses, is tailored to address the specific needs and challenges of his audience. By providing valuable and actionable insights, Flynn has cultivated a loyal following and established himself as a trusted authority in the online business space.

3. Consistent Messaging And Visuals

Consistency is key to building a recognizable and trustworthy personal brand. This consistency should extend to your messaging, visuals, and overall content strategy. Ensure that your brand voice, tone, and style are uniform across all platforms and touchpoints.

Illustrative Example: Neil Patel

Neil Patel, a digital marketing expert, has built his personal brand through consistent messaging and visuals. Patel's brand is characterized by his focus on data-driven marketing strategies and practical tips for growing businesses online.

Patel's website, blog, and social media profiles all feature a cohesive visual identity, including a distinct color scheme and logo. His content consistently reflects his expertise in digital marketing, providing valuable insights and actionable advice. This consistency has helped Patel establish a strong and recognizable personal brand.

Crafting Your Brand Story

Your brand story is a powerful tool for connecting with your audience on an emotional level. It's the narrative that communicates who you are, where you come from, and what you stand for. A compelling brand story can differentiate you from others in your field and create a deeper bond with your audience.

Elements Of A Compelling Brand Story

1. Origin Story: Share the journey that led you to where you are today. This could include your background, challenges you've faced, and pivotal moments that shaped your path.

2. Mission and Vision: Clearly articulate your mission and vision. What do you aim to achieve, and how do you plan to make a difference in your field?

3. Values and Beliefs: Highlight the core values and beliefs that guide your actions and decisions. These elements help your audience understand what you stand for and why.

4. Personal Anecdotes: Include personal anecdotes and stories that illustrate your experiences and lessons learned. These anecdotes make your brand story relatable and engaging.

Illustrative Example: Elon Musk

Elon Musk, the CEO of Tesla and SpaceX, has crafted a compelling brand story that resonates with a global audience. Musk's origin story includes his early life in South Africa, his move to the United States, and his entrepreneurial journey with ventures like Zip2, PayPal, and eventually Tesla and SpaceX.

Musk's mission and vision are centered around advancing technology and making humanity a multi-planetary species. His core values include innovation, sustainability, and pushing the boundaries of what is possible. Musk often shares personal anecdotes, such as the challenges he faced during the early days of Tesla and SpaceX, which add depth and authenticity to his brand story.

Building Your Online Presence

Once you have defined your personal brand, it's essential to build a strong online presence to reach and engage your audience. This involves leveraging various digital platforms and tools to share your content, connect with your audience, and grow your brand.

1. Website And Blog

Your website is the central hub of your online presence. It's where you showcase your brand, share your content, and provide information about your products or services. A blog is an effective way to regularly publish valuable content that attracts and engages your audience.

Illustrative Example: Tim Ferriss

Tim Ferriss, the author of "The 4-Hour Workweek," has built a comprehensive website and blog that serve as the cornerstone of his personal brand. Ferriss's website features a wealth of content, including blog posts, podcasts, and resources on productivity, entrepreneurship, and personal development.

Ferriss's blog posts are in-depth and provide valuable insights and practical advice. By consistently sharing high-quality content, Ferriss has built a loyal following and established himself as a thought leader in his field.

2. Social Media Platforms

Social media platforms are powerful tools for building your personal brand and engaging with your audience. Each platform has its unique features and user base, so it's important to choose the ones that align with your brand and audience.

Illustrative Example: Liza Koshy

Liza Koshy, a comedian and actress, has leveraged social media platforms like YouTube, Instagram, and TikTok to build her personal brand. Koshy's content is characterized by her humor, creativity, and relatable personality.

On YouTube, Koshy posts comedy sketches, vlogs, and collaborations with other creators. Her Instagram feed showcases her vibrant and fun personality, while her TikTok videos feature quick, entertaining clips that resonate with her audience. By leveraging multiple platforms, Koshy has expanded her reach and built a diverse and engaged following.

3. Email Marketing

Email marketing is a valuable tool for nurturing your relationship with your audience. By building an email list, you can communicate directly with your subscribers, share exclusive content, and promote your products or services.

Illustrative Example: Ann Handley

Ann Handley, a digital marketing expert, has built a strong personal brand through her engaging and informative email newsletters. Handley's newsletters are known for their high-quality content, practical tips, and personal touch.

Handley uses her email list to share valuable insights, announce upcoming events, and promote her books and courses. Her newsletters have become a trusted source of information for her audience, further strengthening her personal brand.

Engaging with Your Audience

Engagement is a critical aspect of building a successful personal brand. It's not enough to simply share content; you need to actively interact with your audience and foster a sense of community. Here are some strategies for engaging with your audience:

1. Respond To Comments And Messages

Taking the time to respond to comments and messages shows your audience that you value their input and appreciate their support. This interaction helps build a stronger connection and fosters loyalty.

Illustrative Example: Simone Giertz

Simone Giertz, a YouTuber known for her humorous and inventive robots, is highly engaged with her audience. Giertz regularly responds to comments on her videos, interacts with fans on social media, and participates in live Q&A sessions.

This level of engagement has created a close-knit community of fans who feel personally connected to Giertz. Her responsiveness and authenticity have contributed to her strong personal brand and dedicated following.

2. Create Interactive Content

Interactive content, such as polls, quizzes, and live streams, encourages audience participation and fosters a sense of community. It allows you to gather feedback, learn more about your audience, and create a more engaging experience.

Illustrative Example: Markiplier

Markiplier, a popular YouTuber and gamer, frequently creates interactive content for his audience. He hosts live streams where he plays games and interacts with viewers in real-time, conducts polls to let fans decide on upcoming content, and engages in challenges and collaborations.

This interactive approach has helped Markiplier build a highly engaged and passionate community. His audience feels involved in the content creation process, which strengthens their connection to his personal brand.

3. Host Events And Meetups

Hosting events and meetups, whether in-person or virtual, provides an opportunity to connect with your audience on a deeper level. These events allow you to interact with your fans, share your expertise, and build stronger relationships.

Illustrative Example: Tony Robbins

Tony Robbins, a motivational speaker and author, hosts large-scale events and seminars where he engages with his audience in a dynamic and interactive setting. Robbins's events are known for their high energy, practical insights, and transformative experiences.

By hosting events, Robbins has created a powerful platform for connecting with his audience and building a strong personal brand. Attendees leave these events feeling inspired and motivated, further solidifying their loyalty to Robbins's brand.

Leveraging Your Personal Brand for Business Success

Once you have established a strong personal brand and built a loyal audience, you can leverage your brand for business success. There are several ways to monetize your personal brand and create multiple income streams:

1. Sponsored Content And Brand Partnerships

As your personal brand grows, you may attract opportunities for sponsored content and brand partnerships. These collaborations involve promoting a brand's products or services in exchange for compensation.

Illustrative Example: Zoella

Zoe Sugg, known as Zoella, is a beauty and lifestyle influencer who has successfully leveraged her personal brand for sponsored content and brand partnerships. Sugg collaborates with beauty and fashion brands to create sponsored videos, blog posts, and social media content.

Her authenticity and engaging personality have made her a sought-after influencer for brand collaborations. These partnerships not only provide a significant source of income but also enhance her credibility and reach.

2. Selling Products And Services

Another way to monetize your personal brand is by selling your own products or services. This could include physical products, digital products, online courses, consulting services, and more.

Illustrative Example: Michelle Phan

Michelle Phan, a beauty influencer and entrepreneur, has successfully built a personal brand that extends into her own product lines. Phan started by creating makeup tutorials on YouTube, which garnered millions of views and a massive following.

Leveraging her personal brand, Phan co-founded the beauty subscription service Ipsy and launched her own makeup line, EM Cosmetics. These ventures have been highly successful, generating significant revenue and further establishing Phan's influence in the beauty industry.

3. Affiliate Marketing

Affiliate marketing involves promoting products or services from other companies and earning a commission for each sale made through your referral link. This can be a lucrative way to monetize your personal brand, especially if you have a loyal and engaged audience.

Illustrative Example: Pat Flynn

Pat Flynn, mentioned earlier for his strong personal brand, is also a successful affiliate marketer. Flynn promotes various tools and resources related to online business and entrepreneurship on his website and podcast.

By providing honest reviews and valuable insights, Flynn has built trust with his audience, making them more likely to purchase products through his affiliate links. This trust has translated into significant affiliate income, showcasing the power of a well-established personal brand.

Conclusion

Building a personal brand is a dynamic and multifaceted process that requires authenticity, consistency, and strategic effort. Your personal brand is your most valuable asset in the digital marketing landscape, serving as the foundation for building a loyal community and achieving business success.

By defining your brand identity, curating an authentic voice, and engaging with your audience, you can create a powerful personal brand that resonates deeply and stands the test of time. As you continue to grow and evolve, your personal brand will open doors to new opportunities, partnerships, and income streams, allowing you to build a thriving and sustainable business.

In the next chapter, we will delve deeper into the strategies and tactics for content creation, exploring how to produce engaging and valuable content that attracts and retains your audience. Let's continue this journey towards mastering the art of digital marketing and unlocking your full potential in the digital world.

PART 2: SOCIAL MEDIA PLATFORMS

In the digital marketing ecosystem, social media platforms are your primary channels for reaching and engaging with your audience. Each platform offers unique features, opportunities, and challenges, making it essential to understand how they work and how to leverage them effectively. In this chapter, we'll explore three of the most influential social media platforms in great detail: TikTok, Instagram, and YouTube. We'll also discuss the importance of using multiple platforms to maximize your reach and impact.

TikTok: The Viral Sensation

TikTok has rapidly become one of the most popular

social media platforms, particularly among younger audiences. Its unique format and algorithm make it an exciting and dynamic platform for content creators.

How Tiktok Works

TikTok is primarily a short-form video platform, with videos ranging from 15 seconds to 3 minutes. However, there has been some push to create videos up to 10 minutes long. The app's design encourages creativity and spontaneity, with a wide range of editing tools, filters, and music options available directly within the platform.

Algorithm and Virality

One of TikTok's standout features is its powerful algorithm, which is designed to surface content based on user engagement rather than the number of followers. This means that even new creators have a chance to go viral if their content resonates with viewers. The algorithm takes into account factors such as video completion rate, likes, shares, comments, and the use of trending sounds and hashtags.

However, the TikTok algorithm is constantly evolving, creating both opportunities and challenges for creators. Staying up-to-date with the latest trends and algorithm changes is crucial for maintaining and growing your reach on the platform.

TikTok Shop

TikTok has introduced a feature called TikTok Shop, which allows creators to promote and sell products directly through the app. This feature eliminates the need for creators to proactively reach out to brands, as they can promote any product listed on the TikTok Shop.

Here's how the TikTok Shop works:

1. Product Listings: Brands and merchants list their products on the TikTok Shop.
2. Promotion by Creators: Creators can select products from the TikTok Shop to promote in their videos.
3. In-Video Shopping: Viewers can click on product links within the video to purchase directly, without leaving the app.
4. Commissions: Creators earn a commission on sales generated through their promotional content.

This integration makes TikTok an attractive platform for both creators and brands, providing a seamless shopping experience for users and a monetization opportunity for influencers.

Instagram:

The Old-School Powerhouse

Instagram is one of the most established social media platforms, known for its visual-centric content and loyal user base. While it may be harder to grow on Instagram compared to TikTok, the platform's followers are often seen as more valuable by brands.

How Instagram Works

Instagram offers a variety of content formats, including photos, videos, Stories, Reels, and IGTV. Each format serves a different purpose and can be used strategically to engage with your audience.

Photos and Videos

Traditional posts on Instagram can be either photos or videos, with captions that can include hashtags and mentions. These posts appear in your followers' feeds and can also be discovered through the Explore page.

Stories

Instagram Stories are short, ephemeral posts that disappear after 24 hours. They are a great way to share behind-the-scenes content, daily updates, and interactive elements like polls and questions. Stories appear at the top of the Instagram app and are a popular feature for maintaining daily engagement with your audience.

Reels

Reels are Instagram's answer to TikTok's short-form videos. They are 15 to 30-second clips that can be edited with music, effects, and transitions. Reels have their own dedicated section within the app and are also integrated into the Explore page, offering significant reach potential.

IGTV

IGTV is Instagram's platform for longer-form video content, allowing videos up to 60 minutes long. This feature is ideal for more in-depth content such as tutorials, interviews, and series.

Algorithm and Growth

Instagram's algorithm prioritizes content based on user engagement, relevance, and relationships. Factors such as likes, comments, shares, and saves all contribute to how your content is ranked. Consistent posting, using relevant hashtags, and engaging with your audience are key strategies for growth on Instagram.

While it may be more challenging to grow quickly on Instagram compared to TikTok, the platform's followers are often more engaged and loyal. Brands value Instagram followers highly, making it a lucrative platform for influencer partnerships and sponsored content.

YouTube: The Long-Form Giant

YouTube is the go-to platform for long-form video content. It has a massive user base and offers significant opportunities for monetization through ads, sponsorships, and memberships.

How Youtube Works

YouTube allows creators to upload videos of virtually any length, from a few seconds to several hours. The platform supports a wide range of content types, including vlogs, tutorials, reviews, and live streams.

Long-Form Content

YouTube's strength lies in its capacity for long-form content. This allows creators to dive deep into topics, provide detailed tutorials, and create series or episodic content. Long-form videos tend to generate higher engagement and watch time, which are crucial metrics for YouTube's algorithm.

YouTube Shorts

In response to the popularity of short-form video content, YouTube introduced YouTube Shorts. Shorts are 15 to 60-second vertical videos that appear in a dedicated section within the app. This feature aims to capture some of the audience drawn to platforms like TikTok and Instagram Reels.

Algorithm and Discoverability

YouTube's algorithm considers factors such as watch time, video quality, user engagement, and relevance. Videos with higher watch time and engagement are more likely to be recommended and appear in search results. Consistency, SEO optimization, and compelling thumbnails and titles are essential for success on YouTube.

Monetization

YouTube offers various monetization options for creators:
- *Ad Revenue*: Creators earn a share of the revenue generated from ads shown on their videos.
- *Sponsorships*: Brands pay creators to feature their products or services in videos.
- *Channel Memberships*: Viewers can pay a monthly fee to access exclusive content and perks.
- *Super Chat and Super Stickers*: Viewers can purchase highlighted messages and stickers during live streams.

Because YouTube videos tend to have longer watch times and higher engagement, the platform offers some of the most valuable ad space for advertisers. This makes YouTube an attractive platform for brands and a lucrative opportunity for creators.

The Synergy of Multiple Platforms

While focusing on one platform can be effective, leveraging multiple platforms can maximize your reach and impact. Each platform offers unique opportunities and can drive traffic to others, creating a synergistic effect.

Cross-Posting And Repurposing Content

One of the advantages of using multiple platforms is the ability to repurpose content. However, it's essential to adapt your content to suit the style and audience of each platform.

Illustrative Example: Fitness Influencer

Imagine you're a fitness influencer creating a workout video. Here's how you can repurpose and cross-post this content across multiple platforms:
- *TikTok*: Create a short, engaging clip of the workout with trending music and effects.
- *Instagram*: Post a photo from the workout session with a detailed caption and relevant hashtags. Share snippets in Stories and a longer version in IGTV.
- *YouTube*: Upload the full workout video with in-depth instructions and additional tips.

By tailoring your content to each platform, you can reach different segments of your audience and maximize engagement.

Illustrative Example: Beauty Influencer

Let's consider a beauty influencer who creates a makeup tutorial. Here's how they can repurpose and cross-post the content:
- *TikTok*: Share quick tips and transformations using trending sounds and effects.
- *Instagram*: Post a high-quality photo of the finished look with product details in the caption. Share step-by-step clips in Stories and a longer tutorial in IGTV.
- *YouTube*: Upload a detailed tutorial with product reviews, application techniques, and additional beauty tips.

By customizing the content for each platform, the beauty influencer can engage with their audience in multiple ways, driving traffic and building a cohesive brand presence.

Driving Traffic Between Platforms

Using multiple platforms also allows you to drive traffic from one to another. For example, you can promote your YouTube videos on Instagram Stories, share TikTok clips on Twitter, or embed your Instagram posts in your blog.

Illustrative Example: Travel Blogger

If you're a travel blogger, you can use Instagram to showcase your latest destinations, drive traffic to your YouTube channel for detailed travel vlogs, and use Pinterest to share travel guides and itineraries. Each platform supports the other, enhancing your overall reach and engagement.

Illustrative Example: Tech Reviewer

A tech reviewer can leverage multiple platforms to maximize their reach. For instance, they can:
- *TikTok*: Post quick gadget reviews and tech tips using trending sounds and effects.
- *Instagram*: Share high-quality photos and short videos of the latest gadgets with detailed captions. Use Stories for unboxings and behind-the-scenes content.
- *YouTube*: Upload in-depth reviews and comparisons, providing comprehensive insights and demonstrations.

By utilizing each platform's strengths, the tech reviewer can engage with a broader audience and drive traffic across their channels.

Conclusion

Understanding how different social media platforms work and how to leverage their unique features is crucial for digital marketing success. TikTok offers unparalleled opportunities for virality and product promotion through the TikTok Shop. Instagram, while more challenging to grow on, provides a highly engaged and valuable audience for brands. YouTube's long-form content and diverse monetization options make it an essential platform for building a sustainable and lucrative personal brand.

By strategically using multiple platforms and repurposing content, you can maximize your reach, engage with different segments of your audience, and create a cohesive and impactful online presence. In the next chapter, we will explore the strategies and tactics for content creation, focusing on how to produce engaging and valuable content that attracts and retains your audience. Let's continue this journey towards mastering the art of digital marketing and unlocking your full potential in the digital world.